Egypt

Sue Townsend and Caroline Young

Heinemann
LIBRARY

www.heinemann.co.uk/library
Visit our website to find out more information about **Heinemann Library** books.

To order:
 Phone 44 (0) 1865 888066
 Send a fax to 44 (0) 1865 314091
Visit the Heinemann Bookshop at www.heinemann.co.uk/library to browse our catalogue and order online.

First published in Great Britain by Heinemann Library, Halley Court, Jordan Hill, Oxford OX2 8EJ, part of Harcourt Education.

Heinemann is a registered trademark of Harcourt Education Ltd.

© Harcourt Education Ltd 2003
The moral right of the proprietor has been asserted.

Editorial: Nancy Dickmann, Andrew Solway and Jennifer Tubbs
Design: Jo Hinton-Malivoire and Tinstar Design Limited (www.tinstar.co.uk)
Illustrations: Nicholas Beresford-Davies
Picture Research: Catherine Bevan
Production: Séverine Ribierre

Originated by Dot Gradations Ltd
Printed in China
by Wing King Tong

ISBN 0 431 11726 8
07 06 05 04 03
10 9 8 7 6 5 4 3 2 1

British Library Cataloguing in Publication Data
Townsend, Sue & Young, Caroline
Egypt. – (A World of Recipes)
641.5'123'0962
A full catalogue record for this book is available from the British Library.

Acknowledgements
The publishers would like to thank the following for permission to reproduce photographs: Corbis: p. 5; Gareth Boden: all other photographs.

Cover photographs reproduced with permission of Gareth Boden.

The publishers would like to thank Wafa Iskander for her assistance with the preparation of this book.

Every effort has been made to contact copyright holders of any material reproduced in this book. Any omissions will be rectified in subsequent printings if notice is given to the publishers.

Contents

Key

* easy

** medium

*** difficult

Words appearing in the text in bold, **like this**, are explained in the glossary.

Egyptian food

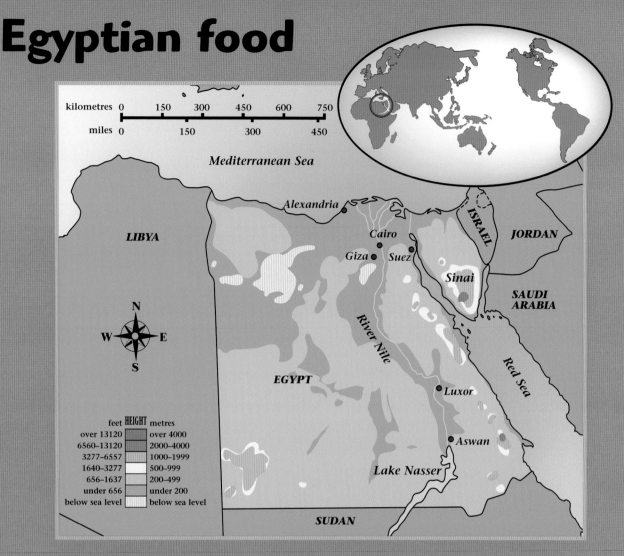

kilometres 0   150   300   450   600   750

miles 0   150   300   450

Mediterranean Sea

Alexandria

LIBYA

ISRAEL   JORDAN

Cairo

Giza   Suez

Sinai

SAUDI ARABIA

N
W   E
S

River Nile

Red Sea

EGYPT

Luxor

Aswan

Lake Nasser

feet HEIGHT metres	
over 13120	over 4000
6560–13120	2000–4000
3277–6557	1000–1999
1640–3277	500–999
656–1637	200–499
under 656	under 200
below sea level	below sea level

SUDAN

Egyptian food

Egypt is in the north-east corner of Africa. It is part
of the world called the Middle East. Egypt is very
dry, and about 96 per cent of the land is desert. The
peoples of the Middle East share many customs and
cooking styles, but all have their own, rich traditions.

In the past

About 5000 years ago, the ancient Egyptians built up
a great civilization. Massive stone pyramids were built
as tombs for the Egyptian kings, called pharaohs, and
some still stand today. After about 3000 years, the
pharoahs' power faded, and in the 1st century BC,
Egypt became part of the Roman Empire. After the
collapse of Roman rule, the following centuries saw

Arab princes, Turkish Ottoman emperors, the French leader, Napoleon Bonaparte, and the British all ruling Egypt at different times. Today, Egypt is called the Arab Republic of Egypt, and most of its people follow the Muslim religion.

Fruit and vegetables are sold in this weekly Egyptian market.

Around the country

Deserts cover most of Egypt, except for a small, **fertile** strip of land along the River Nile. The Nile Delta (the triangular area of land where the Nile flows to the Mediterranean Sea) is especially important for its farmland. Most Egyptians live by farming the land near the river, and catching fish in its waters. When the River Nile overflows its banks in late summer, it floods the land around it. As the floodwater goes down, it leaves behind a layer of rich soil that is good for planting crops. Egyptian farmers grow many kinds of fruit, including dates, grapes and apricots. They also grow grains, such as barley, wheat and rice, and many kinds of vegetables as well.

Egyptian meals

Because it is so hot in the middle of the day, people in Egypt usually eat their main meal mid-afternoon. Breakfast might be yoghurt, bread and fruit, and lunch a selection of small dishes called *mezzeh* (pronounced *mezz-uh*), served with plenty of bread. In villages, several dishes are put in bowls in the centre of a low table. People sit on cushions, helping themselves to some of each dish. Supper is usually a light meal of yoghurt, semit, eggs and fruit.

5

Ingredients

rose water

lemons

melon

mint

pomegranates

almonds

pine nuts

tahini

dates

pistachios

sesame seeds

cinnamon

cumin

fava beans

Beans

Many Egyptian recipes contain beans, including brown fava beans. Most dried beans must be soaked in cold water overnight, **boiled** for 10 minutes, and then **simmered** until soft before you can use them. Using canned beans saves time. Large supermarkets and health food shops sell dried and canned beans.

Cinnamon

Cinnamon comes from the bark of a tree. It has a warm, spicy flavour and is often added to sweet dishes, such as pastries. You can buy it in sticks (which are the curled-up tree bark), or **ground**.

Cumin

Cumin is a spice used to flavour savoury dishes. We know that Egyptian cooks used cumin more than 3000 years ago, because **archaeologists** found some at the pyramids. Buy it as seeds, or ground, from supermarkets.

Dates

The sweet, brown fruits of the date palm tree are called dates. They have a stone in them. Many supermarkets sell fresh dates in winter, and dried dates all year round.

Nuts

Some Egyptian recipes use almonds, which you can buy blanched (without their skins), **flaked**, ground or **chopped**. Others use green pistachio nuts, or pine nuts. Supermarkets sell them all.

Pomegranates

The pomegranate fruit is in season from October to December. Pomegranates have a tough skin and lots of bittersweet, fleshy seeds inside. Large supermarkets sell them when they are in season.

Rose water

Rose water is a delicately scented liquid made from the petals of roses. Look for it in health food shops or chemists. If you cannot find it, use almond essence or orange flower water instead.

Sesame seeds

Sesame seeds add a nutty flavour to dishes, especially when **toasted**. The seeds are also made into sesame oil, which adds a strong, rich flavour when used for **frying**. Buy sesame seeds and sesame oil from supermarkets.

Tahini

Tahini is a stiff paste made by mixing ground, toasted sesame seeds with sesame oil or olive oil. Stir it before you use it. Health food shops or supermarkets sell tahini.

Before you start

Kitchen rules

There are a few basic rules you should always follow when you are cooking:

- Ask an adult if you can use the kitchen.
- Some cooking processes, especially those involving hot water or oil, can be dangerous. When you see this sign, take extra care or ask an adult to help.
- Wash your hands before you start.
- Wear an apron to protect your clothes.
- Be very careful when you use sharp knives.
- Never leave pan handles sticking out, in case you knock them.
- Use oven gloves to lift things in and out of the oven.
- Wash fruits and vegetables before you use them.
- Always wash chopping boards very well after use, especially after chopping raw meat, fish or poultry.
- Use a separate chopping board for onions and garlic, if possible.

How long will it take?

Some of the recipes in this book are quick and easy, and some are more difficult and take longer. The strip across the right-hand side of each recipe page tells you how long it takes to prepare a dish from start to finish. It also shows how difficult it is to make – each recipe is * (easy), ** (medium) or *** (difficult).

Quantities and measurements

You can see how many people each recipe will serve at the top of each right-hand page. You can multiply or divide the quantities if you want to cook for more or fewer people.

Ingredients for recipes can be measured in two different ways. Metric measurements use grams and millilitres. Imperial measurements use ounces and fluid ounces. This book uses metric measurements. If you want to convert these into imperial measurements, see the chart on page 44.

In the recipes you will see the following abbreviations:

tbsp = tablespoon   g = grams   cm = centimetres
tsp = teaspoon   ml = millilitres

Utensils

To cook the recipes in this book, you will need these utensils (as well as essentials, such as spoons, plates and bowls):

- plastic or glass chopping board (much easier to clean than a wooden one)
- food processor or blender
- large frying pan
- 20 cm heavy-based, non-stick frying pan with a lid
- measuring jug
- fish slice
- 600 ml ovenproof dish
- sieve
- small and large saucepans with lids
- set of scales
- sharp knife
- baking sheets
- garlic crusher
- melon-baller
- 23 cm loose-bottomed cake tin
- metal skewers
- baking parchment
- slotted spoon.

 Whenever you use kitchen knives, be very careful.

Broad bean rissoles

This recipe is made slightly differently in each Middle Eastern country. The Egyptian version is called *ta'amiah* (pronounced *ta-mih-ya*), and is made with dried, white broad beans. Use two 440 g cans of the beans and start the recipe at step 3, if you prefer. Serve the rissoles as a snack with salad.

What you need

400 g dried white
    broad beans
2 cloves garlic
1 onion
½ a lemon
1 tsp **ground** cumin
1 tsp ground coriander
½ tsp dried oregano
1 tbsp fresh coriander
1 tbsp tahini
1 tbsp flour
3 tbsp olive oil or
    vegetable oil

To garnish:
fresh coriander leaves

What you do

1 Put the beans into a colander. Rinse them under running cold water.

2 Put them into a bowl and cover with plenty of cold water. Leave the beans to soak overnight. **Drain** and rinse them well.

3 **Blend** the beans in a food processor or blender until coarsely ground.

4 **Peel** and finely **chop** the garlic and onion.

5 Using a lemon squeezer, squeeze the juice from the half lemon.

6 Add the garlic, onion, lemon juice, ground spices, oregano, fresh coriander and tahini to the blender.

7 Blend until the mixture is quite firm and not crumbly (add a little water if necessary).

8 Sprinkle a work surface and your hands with the flour. In your hands, shape 1½ tbsp of the mixture into a ball, and then flatten it with your palm into a teardrop-shaped rissole.

9 Repeat this process with the rest of the mixture.

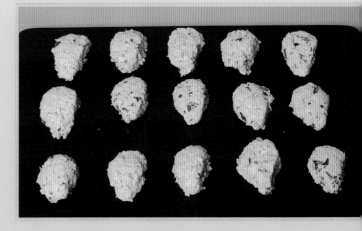

⊘ 10 Heat half of the oil in a large frying pan over a medium heat. **Fry** half the number of rissoles for 3 minutes on each side, until browned.

11 Using a fish slice, lift them on to kitchen paper to drain. Heat the remaining oil and cook the rest of the rissoles.

12 Serve the rissoles hot, garnished with the fresh coriander.

Aubergine dip

Egyptian meals often begin with a selection of small, savoury dishes. They are served to sharpen the diners' appetites, ready for the main course. This aubergine dip is delicious served with warmed pitta bread.

What you need

2 aubergines
2 tsp **ground** cumin
1 clove garlic
1 tbsp lemon juice
4 tbsp tahini
8 pitta breads
1 tbsp chopped
fresh parsley

*To **garnish:***
wedge of lemon

What you do

(!) **1** **Preheat** the oven to gas mark 6/200 °C/400 °F. Put the aubergines on a baking tray, and **bake** for 30 minutes.

(!) **2** **Dry-fry** the cumin in a small frying pan over a medium heat for 30 seconds. Now tip it into a bowl.

3 **Peel** and finely **chop** the garlic. Add it to the cumin with the lemon juice and tahini.

4 When the aubergines are cool, cut them in half. Scoop the flesh into a blender or food processor.

5 Add the cumin and garlic mixture to the blender or processor. **Blend** until smooth.

6 Spoon the mixture into a bowl. **Cover** with clingfilm, and **chill** for 1 hour.

7 **Toast** some pitta breads in a toaster until they are lightly browned.

(!) 8 Using a tea towel to protect your hands from hot steam, lift the pitta breads on to a chopping board. Cut them into wide strips.

9 Repeat steps 7 and 8 with the rest of the pitta breads.

10 Chop the fresh parsley and stir it into the chilled dip. Put the bowl of dip onto a large plate and serve, surrounded by pitta bread strips and garnished with a wedge of lemon.

STARTERS SELECTION

For a really Egyptian selection of starters, try serving Aubergine dip with semit (see page 14), sambusak (see page 16), ta'amiah (see page 10) and some fresh olives.

Semit (Sesame rings)

Street traders in Cairo, the capital city of Egypt, sell freshly made *semit* (pronounced *sem-iht*) as a take-away snack. They are ideal spread with butter, or served with jam or cheese.

What you need

10 g dried yeast
pinch of sugar
150 ml milk
25 g butter
1 tbsp sugar
1 tsp salt
400 g strong plain flour
vegetable oil for
    brushing
1 egg
6 tbsp sesame seeds

What you do

1 Put 90 ml warm water into a jug (if you dip your finger into it, it should feel the same temperature as your finger).

2 Stir in the yeast and a pinch of sugar until they **dissolve**. Leave the jug somewhere warm for 20 minutes.

3 Warm the milk in a saucepan. Add 50 ml water, butter, sugar and salt, and stir. Pour this mixture into a large bowl. When it feels 'finger-warm', stir in the yeast mixture.

4 Stir the flour into the liquid with a wooden spoon. Using your hands, make the dough into a soft, but not sticky, ball.

5 Sprinkle a little flour on to a work surface. Stretch the dough out, then fold it in half. Turn it, then stretch it again and fold. **Knead** like this for 5 minutes.

6 Put the dough into a bowl. **Cover** with a tea towel, and leave somewhere warm for 30 minutes.

7 Brush a little oil on to two baking sheets.

8 Knead the dough again for 10 minutes. Divide it into eight pieces.

9 Shape one piece into a sausage shape about 18 cm long. Dip one end in water, pinch the two ends together and shape into a ring. Make seven more rings.

10 **Beat** the egg with 1 tbsp water. Brush it over the dough rings, and sprinkle with sesame seeds.

11 Lay the rings 5 cm apart on baking sheets. Cover with the tea towel, and leave in a warm place for 40 minutes, until doubled in size. **Preheat** the oven to gas mark 8/220 °C/450 °F.

12 **Bake** the dough rings for 12–15 minutes, until they are golden.

13 Lift them on to a wire rack to cool. Serve straightaway, or keep in an airtight container.

15

Cheese and egg pastries

In Egypt, people often make their own soft cheese. It tastes a little like the Greek cheese, feta. Use feta cheese to make these pastries, called *sambusak* (pronounced *sam-buh-sak*) in Egypt.

What you need

For the filling
1 egg
100 g feta cheese

For the pastry
80 g butter
6 tbsp olive oil
½ tsp salt
225 g plain flour
2 tbsp plain flour
   (for sprinkling on baking sheets and work surface)
1 egg
2 tbsp sesame seeds

What you do

(!) **1** Make the filling first. Put the egg into a small pan of water. Bring to the **boil**, and boil for 8 minutes.

2 Using a slotted spoon, lift the egg into cold water, and leave it to cool.

3 Peel off the shell. Put the egg and feta cheese into a small bowl. Use a knife to **chop** them finely against the side of the bowl, until you have a crumbly mixture.

(!) **4** To make the pastry, melt the butter in a small pan over a low heat. Pour it into another bowl, and add the oil, 6 tbsp water and salt.

5 Stir the flour into the oil mixture until it forms a ball of dough.

6 **Preheat** the oven to gas mark 5/190 °C/375 °F. Sprinkle 1 tbsp flour over two baking sheets.

7 With your hands, shape 2 tbsp of the dough into a ball. Sprinkle a little flour on to a work surface, and roll the ball with a rolling pin until it is an 8 cm circle. Lift each circle on to a baking sheet.

8 Put 1 tsp of the egg mixture into the centre of the circle. Brush a little water around the edge. Fold one side across to the other, and pinch the edges together to make your first pastry.

9 Repeat steps 7 to 9 to make more pastries.

10 **Beat** the second egg, and brush it over each pastry. Sprinkle with sesame seeds.

(!) 11 **Bake** the pastries for 20 minutes, until golden.

12 Cool on a wire rack, and serve hot or cold.

Egyptian bread

On an average day, enough bread is sold in Egypt for each person to have three small loaves. This recipe is for bread called *aiysh* (pronounced *ayesh*) in Egypt. It puffs up when cooked, and is often used for scooping up food.

What you need

7 g sachet easy blend dried yeast
350 g wholemeal flour
100 g strong plain flour

What you do

1 Put the yeast and both kinds of flour into a bowl. Stir them well.

2 Pour 450 ml warm water into a jug (if you dip your finger into it, it should feel the same temperature as your finger).

3 Stir the water into the yeast and flour mixture. Use your hands to make a soft, but not sticky, ball of dough.

4 Sprinkle some flour on to a work surface. Stretch the dough out, then fold it in half. Turn it, then stretch and fold again. **Knead** like this for 10 minutes, until the dough is smooth.

5 Put the dough back into the bowl. **Cover** with a clean tea towel, and leave somewhere warm for 1 hour, until it has doubled in size.

6 Knead the dough on a floured surface for 5 minutes. Cut it into twelve pieces.

7 Using a rolling pin, roll each piece into an 18 cm circle, about ½ cm thick.

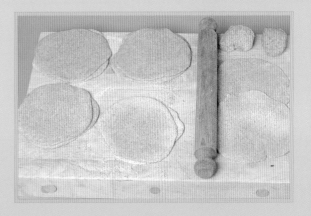

8 Put one circle on top of another, and press the edges together with your fingers. Repeat to make six flat 'loaves'.

9 Put the circles on to baking trays, leaving 5 cm between them.

10 Cover them with a clean tea towel, and leave in a warm place to rise for 40 minutes. **Preheat** the oven to gas mark 6/200 °C/400 °F.

11 Put the baking trays into the oven, and **bake** the bread for 8 minutes, until puffed up and golden.

12 Leave the loaves on the baking trays to cool. Serve the same day.

Onion omelette

People in Egypt eat a lot of eggs. A favourite way of serving them is in an omelette, called an *eggah* in Egypt. They are ideal as a snack or light lunch, with some bread and a salad.

What you need

half an onion
2 eggs
4 tbsp fresh parsley
1 tbsp butter

*To **garnish**:*
sprigs of parsley

What you do

1 **Peel** the half onion and **chop** it.

2 Crack the eggs into a bowl. **Beat** them lightly with a fork. Add salt and pepper.

3 Chop the parsley on a chopping board.

4 Melt the butter in a 20 cm frying pan over a medium heat.

(!) 5 **Fry** the onion over a medium to low heat for about 3 minutes, or until it has softened.

6 Using a slotted spoon, lift half the fried onion into a bowl.

7 Pour the beaten egg into the pan. Tilt the pan so that egg covers the whole of the base of the pan.

8 Cook for 3 minutes until the surface of the egg starts to set.

9 Sprinkle the rest of the cooked onion over the omelette. Fold it in half, using a fish slice.

10 Carefully slide the omelette on to a warmed plate, and serve garnished with fresh parsley.

DIFFERENT FILLINGS
You could add **flaked**, cooked fish, or chopped, cooked chicken, to your omelette, if you wish.

Fattosh (Crunchy salad)

It is so hot during the day in Egypt that people usually only eat a light lunch, such as a salad. This popular salad recipe is called *fattosh* (pronounced *fat-tush*). It uses three fresh herbs, each one adding a slightly different flavour.

What you need

1 cucumber
6 tomatoes
1 bunch spring onions
1 yellow pepper
1 tbsp fresh parsley
1 tbsp fresh coriander
1 tbsp fresh mint
2 or 3 slices of bread
 or pitta breads

For the dressing:
1 clove garlic
4 tbsp olive oil
1 lemon

What you do

1 Trim both ends off the cucumber. Cut it in half lengthways, then into quarters. Cut each quarter into chunks.

2 Cut the tomatoes into quarters, and then into chunks.

3 Trim off the roots and dark green tops of the spring onions. Cut the spring onions into thin **slices**.

4 Cut the pepper in half, throwing away the stalk and the seeds. Cut the flesh into chunks.

5 **Chop** the fresh parsley, coriander and mint finely. Put them and the vegetables you have cut up into a bowl.

6 **Cover** the bowl with clingfilm, and put it in the fridge.

7 Meanwhile, **peel** and crush the garlic in a garlic crusher. Put the garlic into a small, screw-topped jar with the olive oil.

8 Using a lemon squeezer, squeeze the juice from the lemon. Add it, and some salt and pepper to the jar, and screw the lid on tightly.

(!) 9 **Toast** the bread or pitta bread until lightly browned. Tear it into pieces, and **toss** it into the salad. Shake the dressing in the jar.

10 Pour the dressing over the salad and serve.

Goat's cheese and mint salad

Many Egyptian farmers keep goats for their milk and their meat. People drink the milk, or make it into soft, white cheese. Goat's cheese has a strong, tangy flavour that goes well with the fresh salad.

What you need

300 g firm goat's cheese
2 tbsp plain flour
1 egg
50 g fresh breadcrumbs
1 tsp fresh thyme
4 tbsp olive oil

For the salad:
4 tomatoes
1 onion
1 clove garlic
1 tbsp olive oil
6 tbsp fresh mint

What you do

1 Cut the goat's cheese into eight thick **slices**. **Dust** each slice with flour on both sides.

2 **Beat** the egg, and pour it into a shallow bowl.

3 Mix the breadcrumbs and thyme together, and put them on a plate.

4 Dip each slice of cheese into the egg, and then into the breadcrumbs, **coating** them well.

5 Place the coated cheese slices on a plate, and **chill**.

6 Meanwhile, make the salad. **Chop** the tomatoes. **Peel** and finely chop the onion and garlic. Put the tomatoes, onion, garlic and 1 tbsp of olive oil into a bowl.

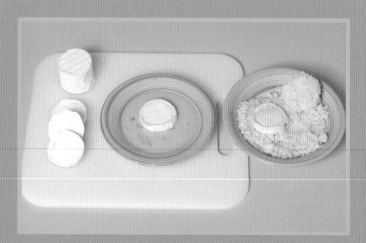

7 Tear the mint leaves and add them to the bowl. **Toss** the salad well and put it on to four plates.

⚠ 8 Put 4 tbsp oil into a frying pan and heat over a medium heat for 1 minute. **Fry** the chilled goat's cheese slices for 2 minutes on each side, until they are golden.

9 Using a fish slice, put two to three slices of cheese on top of each plate of salad. Serve immediately.

AMAZING GOATS

Goats prefer a hot, dry climate, such as that of Egypt. They eat weeds, shrubs and other plants, rather than just grass. Goat's milk is easily digested, and has more **protein** and fat than that of cows.

Fava bean stew

Egyptians cook beans in a tall, thin pot called an *idra* (pronounced *id-rah*). It has a tight-fitting lid, which keeps the steam and moisture in the pot. This stops the beans drying up as they cook.

What you need

300 g dried fava beans
   or other dried beans
4 cloves garlic
2 onions
2 tbsp olive oil
1 tsp **ground** cumin
small pinch ground
   cinnamon
small pinch ground
   allspice
pinch salt
2 tbsp fresh parsley

To garnish:
lemon wedges

What you do

1 Rinse the beans in cold water. Put them in a bowl, cover with plenty of cold water and leave in a cool place overnight.

2 **Drain** the beans. Put them into a saucepan and just cover them with water.

3 Bring to the **boil** and boil for 10 minutes. Now **cover** and **simmer** for 1½ hours, or until the beans are tender. (Add extra boiling water if the beans start to boil dry – you probably do not have an *idra*!)

4 **Peel** and finely **chop** the garlic and onions. Chop the parsley.

5 Heat the oil in a frying pan. **Fry** the garlic and onions over a medium heat until they are golden brown.

6 Stir in the ground spices. Cook for 30 seconds and take the pan off the heat.

(!) **7** Put a colander over a bowl. Drain the beans and tip them back into the pan. Keep the liquid they were cooked in.

8 Stir the spicy onion mixture, salt, parsley and 125 ml of the beans' cooking liquid into the pan. Heat the mixture thoroughly.

9 Cut a lemon into wedges.

10 Spoon the beans on to a serving plate, garnish with lemon wedges and serve with *aiysh* (see page 18), pitta or another sort of bread.

Baked fish with nut sauce

People in Egypt can catch freshwater fish in the River Nile, and sea fish along the country's two, long coastlines. Egyptian cooks may use carp, sea bass, bream or grey mullet for this recipe. You can use cod, haddock or salmon instead. Leave the skin on, to keep the fish firm while it cooks.

What you need

50 g pine nuts
50 g skinned hazelnuts
1 onion
2 tbsp vegetable oil
1 tbsp fresh parsley
411 g can chopped tomatoes
4 fish fillets weighing 75–100 g each (with skin on)
1 tbsp plain flour
1 tbsp butter

To garnish:
fresh parsley

What you do

1 Put the nuts in a small saucepan. Cook them over a medium heat until they start to brown, and then tip them on to a plate.

2 **Peel** and finely **chop** the onion.

(!) 3 Heat 1 tbsp of the oil in a frying pan over a medium heat. **Fry** the onion for 3 minutes, until softened.

4 Chop the parsley. Stir the parsley, tomatoes and nuts into the onions. **Cover** and **simmer** for 5 minutes.

5 **Dust** the fleshy side of the fish with flour.

6 Heat the rest of the oil and the butter in a large frying pan over a medium heat.

(!) 7 Fry the fillets for 3 minutes on each side, until the flesh **flakes** easily.

8 Put the fish on a warmed serving plate. Spoon the tomato and nut sauce over it.

9 Garnish with parsley, and serve with potatoes or rice and some vegetables.

29

Chicken kebabs

Street traders in Egypt sell kebabs tucked into pitta breads as a take-away snack. Egyptian cooks might make them with chicken or pigeon meat. These chicken kebabs would be ideal for cooking on the barbecue in the summer.

What you need

500 g boneless
   chicken portions
  (breast, thigh or leg)
1 onion
1 clove garlic
4 tbsp olive oil
1 lemon
2 tsp paprika

*To **garnish*:*
sprigs of fresh mint
1 tomato

What you do

1 Cut the chicken into 6 cm chunks. Put them in a bowl.

2 **Peel** and finely **chop** the onion and garlic. Add them and the olive oil to the chicken.

3 Wash the lemon thoroughly and cut it into six pieces. Squeeze each piece over the chicken so that the juice goes into the bowl.

4 Stir the lemon skins into the chicken. **Cover** and **chill** for 3 hours.

5 **Preheat** the oven to gas mark 6/200 °C/400 °F. Thread the chicken chunks onto four metal skewers.

6 Sprinkle paprika over the chicken pieces. Lay them on a baking tray.

(!) 7 Cook the chicken in the oven for 20 minutes.

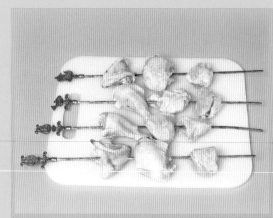

8 **Preheat** a grill to medium hot.

9 **Grill** the chicken pieces for 5–10 minutes until they are golden and crispy.

10 Garnish with mint and a tomato, cut into quarters. Serve the kebabs hot with rice and a salad.

EATING ON THE STREET

The streets of big Egyptian cities echo with the cries of street traders shouting out what they are selling. Many cook the food beside the road. You can buy all sorts of traditional foods without ever needing to go into a restaurant.

Rice with vermicelli

Vermicelli is long, thin strands of pasta, and was first made in Italy. About 600 years ago, traders from the Italian city of Venice visited the Middle East. They introduced vermicelli to the people there. Rice with vermicelli became a traditional Egyptian dish.

What you need

200 g basmati or long grain rice
75 g vermicelli
3 tbsp olive oil
3 tbsp pine nuts

What you do

1 Put the rice into a bowl and cover it with cold water. Leave it for 30 minutes.

2 Tip the rice into a sieve and rinse it under cold water, until the water runs clear.

3 Break the vermicelli into 2 cm pieces.

4 Put a kettleful of water on to **boil**.

(!) 5 Heat the oil in a large saucepan over a medium heat. Add the rice and vermicelli, and stir-**fry** for 2 minutes.

(!) 6 Carefully pour 790 ml of boiling water from the kettle into a measuring jug. Add it to the pan and stir well.

7 Bring the liquid in the pan to the boil. Now turn the heat down to low, put the lid on the pan and **simmer** for 8 minutes.

8 Using a teaspoon, test a little of the rice to see if it is cooked. If it is not, and all the water has been soaked up, add a little extra boiling water.

9 When it is cooked, **drain** the rice, if you need to.

10 Sprinkle the rice with pine nuts and serve with another dish, such as Baked fish in nut sauce (see page 28) or Chicken kebabs (see page 30).

33

Date and nut pastries

Egyptian cakes and pastries tend to be extremely sweet. Many are flavoured with nuts and rose water. In Egypt, people might eat a pastry with a coffee after a meal, or as a quick snack.

What you need

25 g dried dates (with stones removed)
25 g blanched almonds
25 g shelled pistachio nuts
25 g soft brown sugar
½ tsp **ground** cinnamon
125 g unsalted butter
250 g plain flour
1 tbsp rose water, or a few drops of almond essence or orange flower water
2 tbsp milk
icing sugar for **dusting**

What you do

1 **Chop** the dates and nuts into small pieces.

2 Put the dates into a pan with the sugar, cinnamon and 5 tbsp water.

(!) 3 **Cover** and **simmer** for 5 minutes, until the water has been soaked up.

4 Stir in the chopped nuts.

(!) 5 Melt the butter in a pan over a low heat.

6 **Sift** the flour into a bowl. Making cutting movements with a knife, **fold** the melted butter into the flour.

7 Stir in the rose water and milk. Squeeze the mixture into a ball.

8 **Preheat** the oven to gas mark 6/200 °C/400 °F.

9 Cut the dough into sixteen pieces.

10 Roll a piece of dough into a ball. Press your thumb into the ball, and shape the dough around it like a thimble.

11 Put a little of the date and nut filling into the 'thimble'. Press the top edges shut.

12 Put the pastry onto a baking sheet. Use a fork to flatten it slightly, making a pattern on top.

13 Repeat steps 11 and 12 with the other pieces of dough.

14 **Bake** for 10–15 minutes, until golden brown.

15 Cool the pastries on the baking sheet for 10 minutes, and then lift them onto a wire rack. Dust with icing sugar. Serve straightaway, or store in an airtight container.

Um'ali (Pastry pudding)

This Egyptian pudding is made up of layers of nuts, sultanas and spices, and cooked, crushed filo pastry. You can buy ready-made filo pastry in supermarkets. In Egypt, cooks sometimes use toasted bread, or crackers called *raqaq*, (pronounced *ru-cack*) instead.

What you need

50 g butter
150 g filo pastry
40 g dried dates
25 g pine nuts
50 g almonds
25 g pistachio nuts
25 g sultanas
½ tsp **ground** cloves
½ tsp ground cinnamon
¼ tsp ground cardamom
200 g sweetened
 condensed milk
225 ml whipping cream

What you do

1 **Preheat** the oven to gas mark 6/200 °C/400 °F.

2 Melt the butter in a small pan over a low heat.

3 Open the filo pastry and lay it flat. Brush the top sheet with some melted butter, scrunch it up and put it on to a baking sheet (you will need two baking sheets).

4 Repeat this until all the pastry is used.

5 Cook the pastry in the oven for 10 minutes, until lightly browned. Leave to cool.

6 Cut each date in half and take out its stone.

7 Roughly chop the dates and nuts, and put them in a bowl. Add the sultanas and ground spices.

8 Crumble a third of the pastry into a 600 ml ovenproof dish. Sprinkle half the nut mixture on top.

9 Scatter a third of the rest of the pastry on to the nut mixture.

10 Add the remaining nut mixture, and crumble on the rest of the pastry.

(!) 11 Put the condensed milk and cream into a pan. Warm gently over a low heat until the mixture is just **simmering** – no hotter. Pour the liquid over the pastry.

12 Put the dish into the oven and **bake** for 20–30 minutes, until golden. Serve hot.

Date cake

Egyptian cooks use a lot of dates, because they are so plentiful. Dates are very healthy, because they are a fruit, and they are also very sweet. There are more than three hundred different kinds. The most expensive ones are medjool dates, which grow in Egypt.

What you need

Butter or margarine
  for **greasing**
300 g fresh dates
150 g blanched almonds
125 g soft brown sugar
1 orange
4 eggs
25 g caster sugar
½ tsp **ground**
  cardamom
40 g butter
3 tbsp cornflour
1 tsp icing sugar to **dust**

What you do

1 Preheat the oven to gas mark 6/200 °C/400 °F.

2 Spread a little butter or margarine over a 23 cm loose-bottomed cake tin to grease it, and line it with baking parchment.

3 Cut the dates in half and take out the stones.

4 Put the almonds and brown sugar into a blender, and **blend** them until coarsely **chopped**.

5 Now add the dates and blend until finely chopped, but not ground.

6 Using the fine side of a grater, **grate** the rind from the orange.

7 Cut the orange in half. Use a lemon squeezer to squeeze the juice from the half of the orange.

8 Carefully crack open an egg. Keeping the yolk in one half of the shell, let the white drip into a bowl. Pass the yolk from one half of the shell to the other, until all the white has dripped out. Do this for all four eggs. If there is any yolk in the egg white, crack another egg and start again.

9 Whisk the egg whites until they make soft peaks.

10 In a large bowl, **beat** the yolks with the caster sugar and cardamom. Stir in the date mixture, butter, orange rind, 1 tbsp of orange juice and cornflour.

11 Using a large metal spoon, carefully **fold** in the egg whites.

12 Spoon the mixture into the greased tin and **bake** for 35–45 minutes, until the cake springs back when pressed.

13 Cool the cake in the tin for 15 minutes, and then tip out onto a wire rack. Serve on a plate, dusted with icing sugar.

Melon fruit salad with rose water and mint

Farmers around the River Nile can grow many crops, including pomegranates and melons, because the land is criss-crossed with channels carrying water from the river. Rose water and fresh mint make this fruit salad especially refreshing.

What you need

2 small ogen melons
   or any small melons
1 pomegranate
2 kiwi fruit
100 g seedless grapes
1 tbsp rose water or
   a few drops almond
   essence or orange
   flower water
1 tbsp lemon juice
1 tbsp clear honey
6 sprigs of fresh mint

What you do

1 Cut the melons in half. Scoop out the seeds with a spoon and throw them away.

2 Take a melon-baller (or a teaspoon, if you do not have one) and push it into the melon flesh, and twist the handle to make it cut through the flesh and make a ball. Do this to make balls out of the flesh of both melons.

3 Scoop out any melon flesh still left and **chop** it into small pieces. Keep the melon skins.

4 Cut the pomegranate in half, turn it upside down over a large bowl and tap it with a spoon, so that the seeds drop into the bowl.

5 Cut the skin off the kiwi fruit, and cut them into **slices**.

6 Put all the fruit into the bowl with the pomegranate seeds. Add the grapes.

7 In a small bowl, mix the rose water, lemon juice and honey.

8 Rub two sprigs of mint between your fingers, and add them to the rose water mixture. Pour the liquid over the fruit.

9 **Cover** the bowl with clingfilm and **chill** for 1 hour.

10 Using a teaspoon, take out the mint and throw it away.

11 Spoon the fruit into the melon skins, and **garnish** each one with a sprig of mint.

Baked almond-stuffed apricots

Apricots are plentiful in Egypt. People eat them fresh, or dry them to use later. Egyptian cooks use apricots to flavour many savoury dishes as well. If you cannot buy fresh apricots, use four fresh peaches or nectarines instead.

What you need

75 g caster sugar
2 tbsp lemon juice
50 g **ground** almonds
25 g pistachio nuts, shelled
16 fresh apricots
natural yoghurt

What you do

1 **Preheat** the oven to gas mark 5/190 °C/375 °F.

2 Put the caster sugar, lemon juice and 225 ml water into a pan. Heat them gently until the sugar has **dissolved**.

3 Put the ground almonds into a bowl.

4 Roughly chop the pistachio nuts and stir them into the ground almonds. Stir in 2 tbsp of the warm sugary liquid.

5 Cut a slit along the side of each apricot where the skin has a little groove. Gently pull out the stones.

6 Spoon a little nut mixture into the middle of each apricot. Lay the apricots in an ovenproof dish, with the slits facing upwards.

(!) 7 Pour the rest of the sugary liquid over the apricots. Cover the dish with foil and **bake** for 20 minutes.

8 Serve the apricots with a spoonful of the liquid and some natural yoghurt.

YOGHURT AND CHEESE

Natural yoghurt is served with sweet and savoury foods in Egypt. Some people make soft cheese from yoghurt. They pour it into a woven basket over a bowl and wait for the see-through liquid, called whey, to drip through. The thick, milky curds left in the basket are a soft cheese.

Further information

Here are some places to find out more about Egypt and its cooking.

Books

North African Cooking, Hilaire Walden (Apple Press, 1995)
The Complete Middle East Cookbook, Tess Mallos
(Grub Street, 1985)

Websites

http://touregypt.net/recipes
http://www.egyptdailynews.com/recipes/recipes/htm

Conversion chart

Ingredients for recipes can be measured in two different ways. Metric measurements use grams and millilitres. Imperial measurements use ounces and fluid ounces. This book uses metric measurements. The chart here shows you how to convert measurements from metric to imperial.

SOLIDS		LIQUIDS	
METRIC	IMPERIAL	METRIC	IMPERIAL
10 g	¼ oz	30 ml	1 fl oz
15 g	½ oz	50 ml	2 fl oz
25 g	1 oz	75 ml	2½ fl oz
50 g	1¾ oz	100 ml	3½ fl oz
75 g	2¾ oz	125 ml	4 fl oz
100 g	3½ oz	150 ml	5 fl oz
150 g	5 oz	300 ml	10 fl oz
250 g	9 oz	600 ml	20 fl oz
450 g	16 oz		

Healthy eating

This diagram shows you which foods you should eat to stay healthy. Most of your food should come from the bottom of the pyramid. Eat some of the foods from the middle every day. Only eat a little of the foods from the top.

Healthy eating, Egyptian style

Egyptian dishes often include fresh fruit and vegetables, because they grow so plentifully along the River Nile. Most meals include bread, but rice and vermicelli pasta are also popular. Egyptian cooks use eggs, nuts and beans from the middle of the diagram a great deal. They are all good sources of **vitamins**. Traditional cakes can be very sweet, so are only to be eaten in small portions, from time to time.

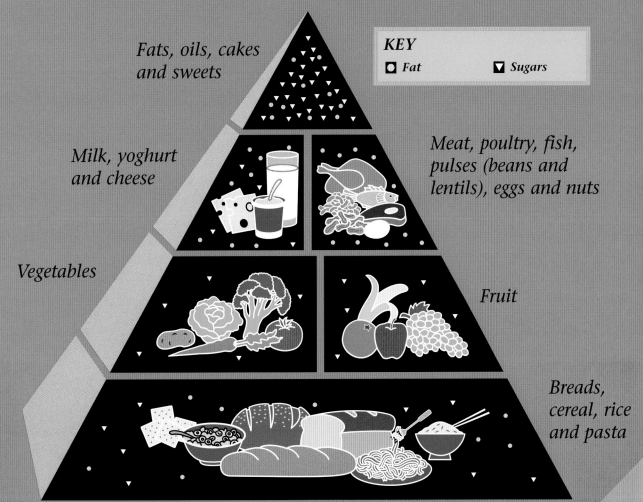

Fats, oils, cakes and sweets

KEY
◻ Fat   ◹ Sugars

Milk, yoghurt and cheese

Meat, poultry, fish, pulses (beans and lentils), eggs and nuts

Vegetables

Fruit

Breads, cereal, rice and pasta

Glossary

archaeologist person who studies the past by looking at objects left behind by earlier peoples

bake cook something in the oven

beat mix ingredients together strongly, using a fork or whisk

blend mix ingredients together in a blender or food processor

boil cook a liquid on the hob. Boiling liquid bubbles and steams strongly.

chill put a dish in the fridge for a while before serving

chop cut into pieces using a sharp knife

coat cover with mixture or sauce

cover put a lid on a pan, or put foil or clingfilm over a dish

dissolve mix something, such as sugar, until it disappears into a liquid

drain remove liquid, usually by pouring something into a colander or sieve

dressing oil and vinegar sauce for salad

dry-fry cook at a high heat without any oil

dust sprinkle with icing sugar or flour

fertile good for growing crops

flake break into flakes

fold mixing wet and dry ingredients by making cutting movements with a metal spoon

fry cook something in oil in a pan

garnish ingredients used to decorate food

grate break something, such as cheese, into small pieces using a grater

greasing spread a little margarine or butter on a baking tray or tin to stop the ingredients sticking when cooked

grill cook under a grill

ground made into a fine powder. If food is coarsely ground, it still has lumps.

knead mix ingredients into a smooth dough, for example for bread. You use your hand to push the dough away from you and then fold it over.

peel remove the skin of a fruit or vegetable

preheat turn the oven on in advance, so that it is hot when you are ready to use it

protein substance found in some food. Living things need it to grow new cells and replace old ones.

sift pass through a sieve

simmer cook liquid on the hob so it bubbles gently.

slice cut into thin flat pieces

toast heat in a pan, oven or, sometimes, under the grill without any oil

toss mix ingredients quite roughly, for example, in a salad

vitamins our bodies get these from food to keep healthy

Index

Titles in the A World of Recipes series include:

Hardback   0431 117268

Hardback   0431 11725X

Hardback   0431 117284

Hardback   0431 117276

Hardback   0431 117306

Hardback   0431 117292

Find out about the other titles in this series on our website www.heinemann.co.uk/library